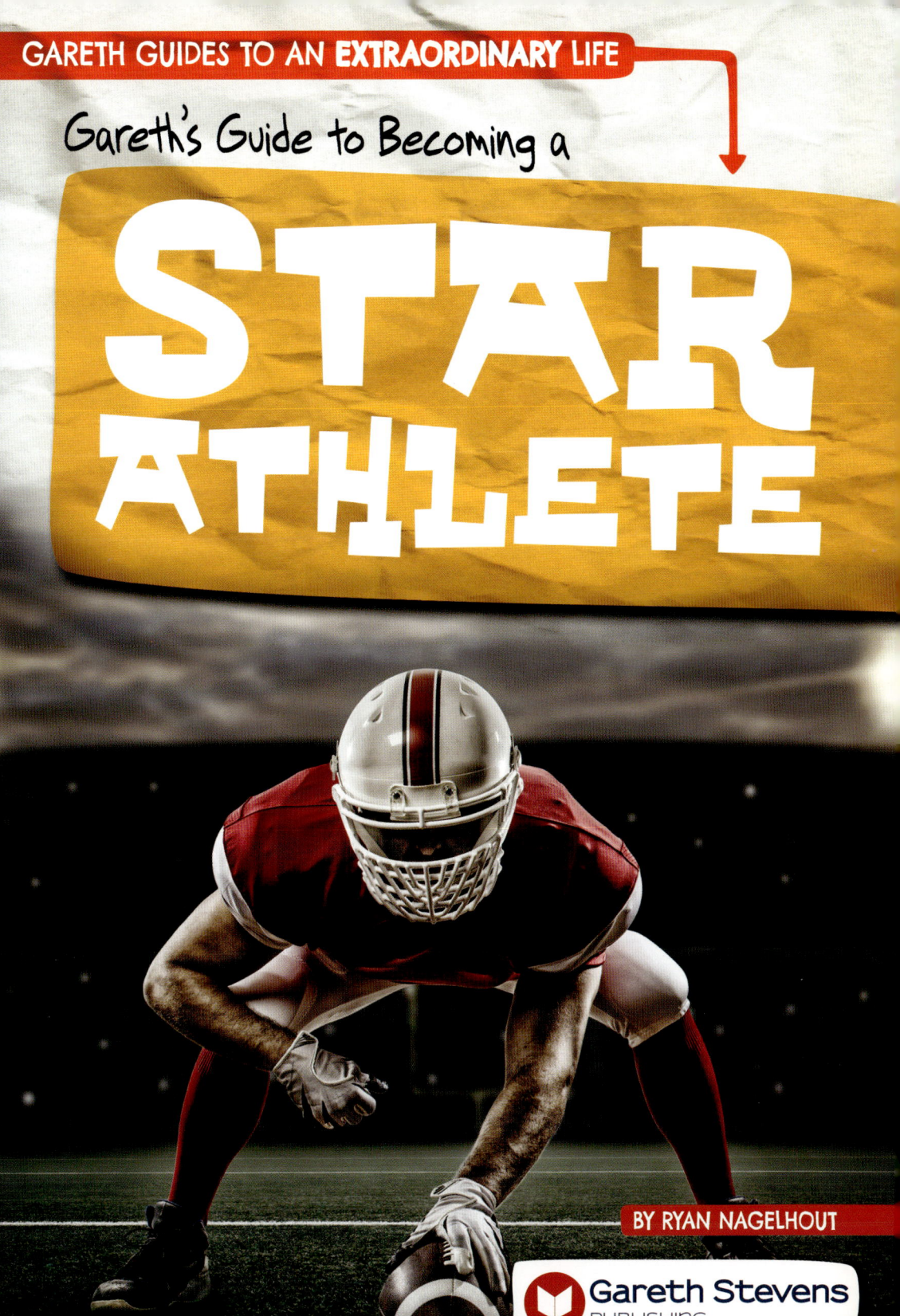

Please visit our website, www.garethstevens.com. For a free color catalog of all our high-quality books, call toll free 1-800-542-2595 or fax 1-877-542-2596.

Cataloging-in-Publication Data

Names: Nagelhout, Ryan.
Title: Gareth's guide to becoming a star athlete / Ryan Nagelhout.
Description: New York : Gareth Stevens Publishing, 2018. | Series: Gareth guides to an extraordinary life | Includes index.
Identifiers: ISBN 9781538203637 (pbk.) | ISBN 9781538203576 (library bound) | ISBN 9781538203361 (6 pack)
Subjects: LCSH: Athletes–Juvenile literature. | Sports–Juvenile literature. | Athletes–Vocational guidance–Juvenile literature.
Classification: LCC GV705.4 N34 2018 | DDC 796–dc23

First Edition

Published in 2018 by
Gareth Stevens Publishing
111 East 14th Street, Suite 349
New York, NY 10003

Copyright © 2018 Gareth Stevens Publishing

Editor: Therese Shea

Photo credits: Cover, p. 1 Beto Chagas/Shutterstock.com; cover, pp. 1–32 (background texture) Thiti Saichua/Shutterstock.com; cover, pp. 1–32 (design elements) VDOVINA ELENA/Shutterstock.com; p. 5 Syda Productions/Shutterstock.com; p. 6 Petr Toman/Shutterstock.com; p. 7 Be Good/Shutterstock.com; p. 8 lev radin/Shutterstock.com; p. 9 picture5479/Shutterstock.com; p. 11 Joseph Sohm/Shutterstock.com; p. 13 Monkey Business Images/Shutterstock.com; p. 15 YanLev/Shutterstock.com; p. 16 Michael Tureski/Icon SMI/Corbis via Getty Images; p. 17 Joe Robbins/Getty Images; p. 19 Ronnie Chua/Shutterstock.com; p. 21 Alex Trautwig/MLB Photo via Getty Images; p. 23 Debby Wong/Shutterstock.com; p. 25 A.RICARDO/Shutterstock.com; p. 27 Tim Clayton/Corbis via Getty Images; p. 29 nik wheeler/Corbis Documentary/Getty Images.

All rights reserved. No part of this book may be reproduced in any form without permission in writing from the publisher, except by a reviewer.

Printed in China

CPSIA compliance information: Batch #CS17GS: For further information contact Gareth Stevens, New York, New York at 1-800-542-2595.

CONTENTS

Work for the Dream 4
Get Out and Play 6
Switch It Up 8
Join a Team 10
Coach 'Em Up 12
School Matters 14
Getting Picked 18
Welcome to the Show 22
Making Money 24
Going for the Gold 26
Rising Stars 28
Glossary 30
For More Information 31
Index 32

WORDS IN THE GLOSSARY APPEAR IN BOLD TYPE THE FIRST TIME THEY ARE USED IN THE TEXT.

WORK FOR THE DREAM

Everyone dreams about what their life will be when they're older. Some want to be a doctor or a teacher. Others plan to be an astronaut or the president. If you love to play sports, you might dream of being a star athlete!

For some, being a star athlete means going pro. If that's your dream, it's never too early to take steps to achieve your goal. It takes years of practice and hard work. Though there are lots of different sports, going pro isn't easy in any of them. The odds are against you. And while it seems like lots of fun, *being* a pro athlete is difficult, too. This guide will tell you the ups and downs of being a sports star. You'll get the knowledge you need before you go pro!

> **SPOTLIGHT!**
> PRO ATHLETES MAKE MONEY, WHILE AMATEUR ATHLETES DO NOT. THEY CAN BE EQUALLY GREAT AT THEIR SPORTS, THOUGH!

Few Chances to Shine

There aren't that many professional sports leagues out there. The most famous in the United States are the "big four"—football (NFL), hockey (NHL), basketball (NBA), and baseball (MLB). For women, there's the WNBA and a few other leagues. But athletes of less popular sports aren't so lucky. If you want to go pro in **cricket**, for example, you'll have to go overseas. Many sports leagues have been started over the years, but not all of them last.

Not all star athletes go pro, but this book will give you some tips that can help you find your own way to athletic greatness!

GET OUT AND PLAY

There's one thing star athletes have in common—they're athletic! That means they're physically fit and know how to train to get stronger. Many doctors and scientists think kids should be active at least 60 minutes a day. Athletic activity helps your heart get stronger, improves your endurance, and keeps you in good shape.

If you want to be a sports star, why not spend those 60 minutes playing sports? You can play in gym class or during recess. You can play soccer in a park after school. You might even get to ice-skate outside and play hockey if you live somewhere cold. Lots of sports are team sports, so gather some friends. Learning to play with others—teamwork—is a big part of succeeding as an athlete.

> **SPOTLIGHT!**
> OLYMPIC SWIMMER MICHAEL PHELPS ONCE SAID HE ATE 12,000 CALORIES PER DAY WHEN TRAINING! MOST ATHLETES NEED MUCH LESS.

Eating for Excellence

Your body needs energy to exercise, and it gets that energy from food. Eating fruits, vegetables, and whole grains is a good place to start. Try not to eat very fatty or sugary foods. Calcium helps build the strong bones that athletes depend on, and iron carries oxygen to muscles. Most kids don't get enough calcium or iron, but they can easily add them to their diet by eating green vegetables, dairy products, and lean meat, fish, and chicken.

Distance Run in a Sports Event

BASEBALL → 0.375 mile (0.6 km)

FOOTBALL → 1.25 miles (2 km)

BASKETBALL → 2.55 miles (4.1 km)

TENNIS → 3 to 5 miles (4.8 to 8 km)

SOCCER → 7 miles (11.2 km)

Some sports stars have to run a long way each game. Could you keep up?

SWITCH IT UP

What sport do you want to be a star in? What about basketball? Soccer? Do you love to skate and think you can play hockey? Well, you don't have to choose right now! Scientists say the best way to get good at sports is by playing a lot of them.

You might think getting really good at one sport is the best way to become a star. That might be true for some, but the skills you learn playing one sport might apply to another you eventually learn to love more. Play as many sports as you can. Working on your golf swing, for example, might help your swing at the plate while playing baseball. So try new things! You never know what sport will become your passion.

▶ SPOTLIGHT!
STEVE NASH PLAYED 18 SEASONS IN THE NBA, BUT HE DIDN'T PICK UP A BASKETBALL UNTIL HE WAS 12 OR 13! HE PLAYED SOCCER GROWING UP AND SAID IT HELPED HIM LATER IN THE NBA.

Play More, Protect Yourself!

Some doctors think children who play one sport a lot are more likely to get hurt. They might use certain body parts over and over again until those parts get worn down and injured. In a Loyola University study of youth athletes, those who only played one sport were 70 to 93 percent more likely to get hurt than those who played more than one. You need to mix it up, or you'll get burned out!

You might love one sport a lot, but make sure you give others a try.

JOIN A TEAM

One of the best parts of sports is playing on a team. Groups such as the Police Athletic League (PAL) or Amateur Athletic Union (AAU) organize sports leagues you might be interested in. Peewee or Pop Warner leagues are great ways to learn football. If you live near a hockey rink, there might be club teams to join.

Even if you play a solo sport such as golf or tennis, you could try out for a team at your school. Joining a team is important because you get to learn all the rules of the game you love. You can also play for great coaches who know the game and can help you become a better player.

21.5 MILLION

→ number of people ages 6-17 playing team sports in the United States

▶ SPOTLIGHT!

ANTWAAN RANDLE EL HAD A LONG NFL CAREER AS A WIDE RECEIVER, BUT HE PLAYED COLLEGE FOOTBALL AS A QUARTERBACK AT INDIANA UNIVERSITY. HE EVEN THREW A TOUCHDOWN PASS IN SUPER BOWL XL!

Pick a Position

Even if you pick one sport, there are decisions to make, like which position to play. In baseball, every position is different. If you can throw the ball very hard, you might be a good pitcher. If you're very fast and good at catching the ball, you might be a center fielder. You should try many different positions early on in your career. It's best if you can play a lot of different roles!

The best way to learn how good you are at a sport is by playing with others. There's lots of information online about local team sports opportunities.

COACH 'EM UP

Pure athletic talent can only get you so far in sports. There's a lot to learn about the sport you love, and a lot of that knowledge comes from coaches. A good coach can see the potential, or promise, in a young athlete and encourages players to work through setbacks as they follow their dreams.

Listening to your coach is important in a game and on the sidelines. A coach guides the team to victories, but also serves as a **mentor** to players. Coaches know how to help young players improve and can help them find the position that suits their skills. If you're very talented, a coach can help you deal with decisions that could impact your chances of competing at a high level.

Work Like KD

Working with a coach you trust can help you get better as a player. Coaches had great impact on NBA superstar Kevin Durant's life. Durant started playing for AAU basketball teams near Washington, DC, when he was 9. Taras Brown, one of his coaches, taught him to dribble around chairs and posts to perfect his ball-handling skills. Durant practiced for hours running up hills and shooting hoops to get faster, stronger, and more exact.

> **→ SPOTLIGHT!**
> DURANT'S AAU COACH KNEW THE FUTURE SUPERSTAR COULD BE SOMETHING SPECIAL. TARAS BROWN REMEMBERED, "I TOLD HIM THAT FIRST YEAR, 'YOU GOT THE GIFT OF WANT-IT-BAD.' HE WASN'T JUST HUNGRY, HE WAS A SPONGE."

You should listen to what a coach has to say, even if they tell you to stop playing. Coaches usually have your best interests in mind!

SCHOOL MATTERS

You've probably heard it before: If you want to play sports, you need good grades. It might sound like a trick to get you to pay attention in class, but it's true! How you do in school can directly affect whether you're allowed to play in high school and your chances of succeeding as an athlete overall. Also, most sports paths go through colleges. You can't get into a college after high school if you don't study and know how to take tests well. And once you get in, you'll likely need to maintain certain grades to play a sport.

You also have to be smart to play sports at a high level. Learning a playbook and **anticipating** the other team's plays while in the game requires brains.

85 — number of **scholarships** each of the 128 Football Bowl Subdivision (FBS) college football teams can offer student athletes

Everyone Struggles Sometime

There's no shame in having a hard time in school, but you should never give up on your grades. Before offensive lineman Michael Oher made the Pro Bowl, he was a student in Memphis, Tennessee, having difficulties in the classroom. People saw Oher's talent on the field and worked with him to get his grades up. With the help of a tutor, Oher was accepted at the University of Mississippi. He played football there and later was **drafted** by the Baltimore Ravens.

> **SPOTLIGHT!**
> OHER'S PATH TO NFL STARDOM WAS THE SUBJECT OF A BOOK BY MICHAEL LEWIS CALLED *THE BLIND SIDE*. IT WAS LATER MADE INTO AN AWARD-WINNING MOVIE OF THE SAME NAME!

Focusing at practice and in the classroom is important for a student athlete who wants to attend college.

15

Some sports stars even go to certain high schools just to improve their chances of playing in the pros. Many hockey players, such as Sidney Crosby and Zach Parise, attended Shattuck-St. Mary's School, a hockey hotbed in Minnesota. Kevin Durant played his junior year at Oak Hill Academy in Virginia to raise his profile and get noticed by colleges.

Many student athletes use sports as a way to attend college. Colleges and universities all across the country offer scholarships to male and female students who excel at many kinds of sports, including basketball, track and field, and even bowling. Colleges also look for students interested in a variety of activities, so playing a sport could help you make it to your dream school anyway!

$2.7 BILLION

scholarship money given to more than 150,000 student athletes each year

Women have fewer opportunities than men to go pro, but some college athletic programs are famous for their female athletes, such as the University of Connecticut Huskies.

Student-Athlete Superstar

Seattle Seahawk cornerback Richard Sherman worked hard in school all his life. Sherman went to Dominguez High in Compton, California. It was a tough place to grow up, but he studied hard and got great grades. Sherman played football and ran track, too. His hard work paid off—he got into Stanford University and played with quarterback Andrew Luck. Both were drafted and play in the NFL.

Richard Sherman is one of the highest-paid defensive backs in the NFL.

SPOTLIGHT!

WHEN RICHARD SHERMAN WAS ACCEPTED TO STANFORD, HE BECAME THE FIRST DOMINGUEZ STUDENT IN MORE THAN 20 YEARS TO GET AN OFFER FROM THE UNIVERSITY!

Getting Picked

If you want to play professional sports, you'll have to play without pay for a while. Most professional leagues have some sort of rule that states when a player can go pro. Some, such as the National Football League and National Basketball Association, say a player can join the league after a set amount of time has passed since high school. Others base their rules on age.

For a player to become **eligible** for the entry draft in the NHL, they must be 18 years old by September 15 of the draft year. In the MLB, you can get drafted after high school or as a college player. But teenagers rarely make the pros, and many teams wait until players graduate from college to sign them to pro contracts.

1 in 5,000

the odds a high school athlete playing a major sport becomes a pro athlete

SPOTLIGHT!
IN 2016, LOUISVILLE QUARTERBACK LAMAR JACKSON WON THE HEISMAN TROPHY FOR COLLEGE FOOTBALL'S BEST PLAYER AT JUST 19 YEARS OLD. HE STILL WASN'T ELIGIBLE FOR THE NFL, THOUGH!

Changing the Game

Rules about when athletes can turn pro are always changing. Basketball players were once drafted out of high school until the NBA changed its rules in 2005. Now players need to be 1 year removed from high school. Many top players go to college for a year and then enter the draft. When college freshmen and sophomores have outstanding football seasons, many wonder if the NFL should change its draft rules to let them enter the league early.

Big Four Age Requirements for Draft Eligibility

NFL → player must be 3 years removed from high school

NHL → player must be 18 years old by September 15 of the draft year

NBA → player must be 19 years old and at least one season must have passed since high school graduation

MLB → player must be 19 years old and at least one season must have passed since high school graduation

Here are the minimum age requirements for some major pro sports leagues.

Most pro sports in the United States have some form of draft. If you're an amateur athlete in college, you have to declare yourself eligible for the draft. That means you want a team to draft you and you won't finish college. You usually sign with an agent, who can help you **negotiate** a contract with a team if you get drafted. When a player gets picked during the draft usually determines how much money they'll make with their first contract.

Each draft is different. There can be up to 40 rounds in Major League Baseball's draft, which has hundreds of picks. The WNBA, meanwhile, picks just 36 players. While most baseball picks never make it to the majors, WNBA picks often make an instant impact on their team.

60 — the number of picks in the NBA Draft each year

> ### ▶ SPOTLIGHT!
> THE BEST ODDS OF MAKING THE PROS ARE IN HOCKEY. STILL, JUST 1 IN 598 HIGH SCHOOL HOCKEY PLAYERS ARE DRAFTED AND APPEAR ON NHL ICE. BASEBALL IS A CLOSE SECOND-HIGH SCHOOL BASEBALL PLAYERS HAVE A 1 IN 659 CHANCE OF PLAYING IN THE PROS.

Long Odds

You might be the best soccer player in your school, but the odds are against you ever making it to the pros. Out of more than 400,000 high school soccer players, just 75 are drafted by Major League Soccer (MLS) each year. That's a 1 in 5,768 chance of a high school athlete going pro in soccer! Women's basketball odds are even worse—you have a 1 in 13,015 chance of making the pros if you played in high school!

Draft day is one of the most exciting days of an athlete's career!

WELCOME TO THE SHOW

Most top players picked in the NBA and NFL drafts sign contracts with and play for pro teams right away. However, not every athlete who gets drafted plays in the pros immediately. Some lower round picks even get cut! You can never be sure you'll play in the pros until you finally step on the field—and you'll never stop working in order to stay there.

In baseball, draft picks can finish their high school careers or go to college. If they sign a professional contract, they'll start playing in the minor leagues. These teams are **affiliated** with a pro team and develop new talent for their major league team. Hockey and basketball have similar systems, with minor or **developmental leagues** to help players gain new skills.

> **SPOTLIGHT!**
> MANY NFL PLAYERS WORRIED ABOUT INJURIES HAVE RETIRED EARLY. BARRY SANDERS AND MARSHAWN LYNCH ARE TWO STAR RUNNING BACKS WHO RETIRED EARLY—SANDERS AT AGE 30 AND LYNCH AT 29.

Women Go Pro

Female athletes have fewer pro sports leagues than men, but some are quite successful. The LPGA (Ladies Professional Golf Association), founded in 1950, is the longest-running women's pro sports organization. The WNBA began in 1996 because of public interest in women's basketball. The Women's Tennis Association (WTA) may be the most popular worldwide. There are also currently women's pro leagues in the United States for softball, lacrosse, and soccer. Canada hosts a women's professional hockey league.

Injuries, younger or better players, and a number of other factors can cut your career in sports short.

MAKING MONEY

How much money do pro athletes actually make? Every athlete's contract is different. Some make tens of millions of dollars a year, while others make much less. According to the US Bureau of Labor and Statistics, the average athlete made $44,680 in 2015. Athletes playing major sports often make much more. The minimum salary in Major League Baseball was $507,500 in 2016.

However, many other pro athletes—such as those in the National Lacrosse League—have full-time jobs and play on the weekends. They make much less money than athletes in the big four sports. John Tavares—the highest-scoring player of all time in the National Lacrosse League—was a math teacher in Canada! He made about $30,000 a year playing for the Buffalo Bandits until he retired in 2015.

> ## SPOTLIGHT!
> THE FIRST PROFESSIONAL FOOTBALL PLAYER WAS WILLIAM "PUDGE" HEFFELFINGER. HE MADE $500 FOR ONE GAME WITH THE ALLEGHENY ATHLETIC ASSOCIATION ON NOVEMBER 12, 1892.

Endorsements

For some athletes, a contract with a pro team is enough money to live on for the rest of their life. Others find they can make more money through **endorsements**. Companies selling food, shoes, and other products sometimes use athletes to advertise. Before LeBron James was drafted in 2003, he signed a $90 million contract with Nike. In 2015, James agreed to a new "lifetime" deal with Nike that's estimated to be worth more than $1 billion!

LeBron James led the Cleveland Cavaliers to win their first NBA championship in 2016.

25

GOING FOR THE GOLD

Not every star athlete goes pro, but they can still compete at the highest level. They can aim for the Olympics! The Olympic Games are sports competitions involving athletes from more than 200 countries. The Olympics are divided into the Summer Games and the Winter Games, which feature sports suitable for those seasons. Each is held in a different country once every 4 years. Athletes compete for medals: gold for first place, silver for second place, and bronze for third place.

Olympic sports are wide ranging, highlighting many sports and athletic skills. The Summer Games include gymnastics, swimming, basketball, boxing, cycling, diving, judo, sailing, soccer, softball, volleyball, water polo, weight lifting, and wrestling. The Winter Games include ice-skating, skiing, speed skating, bobsledding, and the biathlon (skiing and shooting).

776 BC → year of the first Olympic Games, held in Greece

> **SPOTLIGHT!**
> AMERICAN SWIMMER MICHAEL PHELPS HAS WON MORE OLYMPIC MEDALS THAN ANY OTHER ATHLETE—28!

A Sport for Every Athlete

The Olympics remind us there are more sports out there than the ones we see regularly on TV. Don't be discouraged if you're not great at basketball, football, or another popular sport. If you're strong, you might want to check out weight lifting. If you love biking, try a cycling competition. Look on the Internet to find local sports organizations that help you develop your skills and achieve your athletic goals. You can still be a star!

New sports have been added to the Olympics over the years, and women now compete in some events that were once only for men. Though the Olympics were once only for amateur athletes, pros can now compete in some sports as well.

RISING STARS

When sports stars talk to reporters, they love to use clichés! These are overused phrases people say often, such as "we gave 110 percent today" or "we're taking it one game at a time." Athletes use them because they're easy to remember and an easy way to talk about experiences in their sport. But many clichés, while boring, have truth in them! You *do* have to perform your best to succeed, and you *do* have to win many games to get to the championship.

It takes years of training, and maybe a bit of luck, to rise to the top of your sport and be considered a star. The odds might be long, but many succeed in becoming star athletes—why not you?

> ### ▶ SPOTLIGHT!
> ONCE YOU'VE MADE IT, GIVE BACK! LEBRON JAMES, FOR EXAMPLE, LOVES HELPING AT-RISK KIDS IN HIS HOMETOWN OF AKRON, OHIO. WHAT CAUSES WILL YOU HELP WHEN YOU BECOME A SPORTS STAR?

To the Hall

Many sports have a Hall of Fame that inducts, or lets in, the game's greatest players. In sports such as football and baseball, the writers who cover the sport pick who gets into the Hall of Fame. Many great players such as Mark McGwire and Barry Bonds haven't been inducted into the Baseball Hall of Fame because the writers think it's unfair these athletes took **steroids** to get ahead. Your conduct as a star is important, too.

Are you destined to be the "best of the best"? Will you be in a sports Hall of Fame someday? Start on your path to superstardom today!

GLOSSARY

affiliated: belonging to or connected to a larger organization

anticipate: to act before another, often in order to stop or oppose

cricket: a game played with a ball and bat by two sides of usually 11 players each on a large field centering upon two wickets, each defended by a batsman

developmental league: a lower league where players learn new skills and try to earn a spot on a pro team

draft: selecting a player from a pool of potential players entering the league. Also, the process of selecting new players.

eligible: qualified to take part or be chosen

endorsement: money earned for supporting products

mentor: someone who teaches or gives help and advice to a less experienced and often younger person

negotiate: to deal with some matter that requires ability for its successful handling

scholarship: an amount of money that is given by a school to a student to help pay for the student's education

steroid: an illegal drug taken by an athlete to make their body stronger

FOR MORE INFORMATION

Books

Herweck, Diana. *In the Game: An Athlete's Life.* Huntington Beach, CA: Teacher Created Materials, 2013.

Mattern, Joanne. *So, You Want to Work in Sports? The Ultimate Guide to Exploring the Sports Industry.* Hillsboro, OR: Beyond Words, 2014.

Nagelhout, Ryan. *The Science of Football.* New York, NY: PowerKids Press, 2016.

Websites

How to Become a Professional Athlete
kidzworld.com/article/25583-how-to-become-a-professional-athlete
Find out more about what it takes to become a pro sports star.

Let's Move!
letsmove.gov
Learn more about how to get active and develop good health habits.

Publisher's note to educators and parents: Our editors have carefully reviewed these websites to ensure that they are suitable for students. Many websites change frequently, however, and we cannot guarantee that a site's future contents will continue to meet our high standards of quality and educational value. Be advised that students should be closely supervised whenever they access the Internet.

INDEX

AAU 10, 12, 13
baseball 5, 8, 11, 20, 22, 29
basketball 5, 8, 12, 16, 19, 21, 22, 23, 26, 27
coaches 10, 12, 13
draft 18, 19, 20, 21, 22
Durant, Kevin 12, 13, 16
endorsements 25
football 5, 10, 14, 17, 18, 19, 24, 27, 29
golf 8, 10
grades 14, 17
Hall of Fame 29
hockey 5, 6, 8, 10, 16, 20, 22, 23
Jackson, Lamar 18
James, LeBron 25, 28
LPGA 23
minor leagues 22
MLB 5, 18, 20, 24
MLS 21
money 4, 20, 24, 25

Nash, Steve 8
NBA 5, 8, 12, 18, 19, 22, 25
NFL 5, 10, 15, 17, 18, 19, 22
NHL 5, 18, 20
Oher, Michael 14, 15
Olympics 26, 27
PAL 10
Peewee leagues 10
Phelps, Michael 6, 26
Pop Warner leagues 10
Randle El, Antwaan 10
school 6, 10, 14, 16, 17, 18, 19, 20, 21, 22
Sherman, Richard 17
soccer 6, 8, 21, 23, 26
tennis 10
WNBA 5, 20, 23
women 5, 16, 21, 23, 27
WTA 23

32